DATE DUE

especially
HEROES

Written by Virginia Kroll
Illustrated by Tim Ladwig

EERDMANS BOOKS FOR YOUNG READERS

Grand Rapids, Michigan   Cambridge, U.K.

With everlasting love and thanks to my neighbor, Mrs. Hall, to my parents, Lester and Helen Kroll, and to my friends' fathers, Mr. Al Lembke and Mr. Jesse Wilson, heroes in my life and, therefore, of this book.

— *V. K.*

In memory of my father, a hero to me.

— *T. L.*

Text © 2003 by Virginia Kroll
Illustrations © 2003 by Tim Ladwig
Published in 2003 by Eerdmans Books for Young Readers
An imprint of Wm. B. Eerdmans Publishing Company
255 Jefferson S.E., Grand Rapids, Michigan 49503
P.O. Box 163, Cambridge CB3 9PU U.K.

Library of Congress Cataloging-in-Publication Data
Kroll, Virginia L.
Especially heroes / written by Virginia Kroll ; illustrated by Tim Ladwig
p. cm.
Summary: After talking about heroes and martyrs at school, a young girl gets a
first-hand look at heroism when her father and several others protect their neighbor
from a group of racists.
ISBN 0-8028-5221-1 (alk. paper)
[1. Heroes—Fiction. 2. Racism—Fiction.] I. Ladwig, Tim, ill.II. Title.
PZ7.K9227 Es 2003
[E]—dc21
2002009003

The illustrations were created with watercolor, varnish, oil, and pencil on paper.
The type was set in Times.
Book design by Matthew Van Zomeren

I was in fourth grade in 1962. One Tuesday our lesson was about the Revolutionary War, which somehow led to the subject of soldiers in all wars.

Mrs. Brennan asked us how many of our parents were veterans of World War II. Nine kids raised their hands. Eight of them had fathers who had been in the Army, and Sandy Campbell's dad was in the Marines. I raised both hands because my father was an Army veteran, and my mother was a Navy nurse.

Danny Rozbicki said that he had two uncles who were veterans, but they never came home because they were killed overseas.

Mrs. Brennan folded her hands and bowed her head like she was going to say a prayer. "People fight hard for ideals like freedom," she said. "Sometimes heroes die for the things they believe in."

I wondered about that all the way to religion class. In those days, all the kids at Ebenezer Elementary got out of school an hour early every Tuesday and walked to the churches nearby.

My best friend, Babs Wilson, went up the hill to the "red church," and Sandy Campbell went to the "white church" across from the playground, because Babs and Sandy were Protestant. My other friend, Annie Lembke, and I went down the hill to Queen of Heaven because we were Catholic.

And it's weird, because the same day Mrs. Brennan talked about heroes, Sister Agnes Marie talked about martyrs. She clasped her hands, raised her eyes to the ceiling, and whispered, "Martyrs gave their lives to God, and many of them were no older than you children are now. There are even modern day martyrs." She called them "soldiers of Christ."

Even Danny Rozbicki didn't act up that day. Our ears and eyes were wide open when Sister Agnes Marie described how some of the martyrs had died. Then she asked us, "Do any of you love anything so much that you would die for it?"

I slunk down at my desk and was so glad she didn't make us answer, but I wondered about her question for the rest of the religion class. Was there anything that would make me risk my life?

After class I asked Annie, "Do you think you could ever be a soldier of Christ?"

"Nope," she said right away. "But maybe if I cared about something so much . . . " Her voice trailed off.

"I know," I agreed. We got to the gym where the primary kids waited for us to walk them home. My second grade sister, Nancy, joined us before we even saw her.

Suddenly Annie laughed. "I'm sure Donald could be a soldier. Look, Ginny." She pointed at my kindergarten brother. He was crashing his dinosaur figures together and making what Momma called "boy sounds" with his mouth.

"You're right, Annie," I said. "Come on, Donald." I took his hand but he wanted to run ahead on the sidewalk. "Watch the driveways," I called.

"I can't imagine my father being a soldier," I said, going back to that. "He's too . . . too . . ."

"Gentle," Annie finished my sentence. "I mean, he wouldn't hurt a fly."

She was right. Daddy never swatted anything. He even put jars over bugs and took them outside. And when our dog, Pal, got burs stuck in his fur, Daddy picked them out, pricker by sticky pricker, so it wouldn't hurt Pal, even if it took an hour, which it sometimes did.

Once in third grade, Mrs. Tasseff sent a note home about me talking too much in class and missing an assignment because of it. Momma yelled a lot and grounded me. Daddy shook his head softly and knelt down. He put his hands on my shoulders and looked straight with his brown eyes into mine. "I'm disappointed in you, Ginny," he said, which hurt me more than any yelling or grounding ever could. "You'll have to try harder." I did, and I never got another note because I didn't want to see that look in his eyes again.

Babs met us outside the "red church," and we headed down the street. She and Annie reached their houses first. Nancy, Donald, and I had a little farther to go.

Just before we got to our driveway, a familiar voice called out. "Hey, ain't you three a beautiful sight for these old eyes!" It was Mrs. Hall, our next-door neighbor. She had moved here after Mr. Hall died six months before, and she'd become like a grandma to us already. "I got cocoa brewin' and cookies all done up for you. Want some?"

"Yes, please," we chorused.

"Quick. Chico's outta his cage." She hustled us in. Chico was Mrs. Hall's perky little parakeet. Once he flew out the window and all she did was cry till Mr. Schultz caught him in a net two days later.

"Your mama's plum tuckered out. So I said to her, 'Go on Helen, you just lay that head down and get some sleep. I'll be pleased to tend them honey-children for you after school.'" I loved the sound of her voice and how she called us "honey-children."

We put our book bags and lunch boxes on the floor and slid into the chairs around Mrs. Hall's comfy table. Chico came and perched on her shoulder while Mrs. Hall hummed in deep, gold tones, setting out oatmeal-raisin cookies and filling our mugs.

Nancy made a "click" with her tongue, so Chico flew down and sat on her head. Mrs. Hall said, "Don't he know a bird lover when he sees one, ain't that so? Now, what'd you all learn about today?" she asked, joining us at the table.

Nancy told her about how mealworms eat potatoes and then turn into beetles. I told her about soldiers and heroes and martyrs and asked her the same question Sister Agnes Marie had asked us: Do you love anything so much that you would die for it? Mrs. Hall answered, "I believe I do, honey-child. I believe so." I waited, but she never told me what it was.

Donald was playing with his dinosaurs again when tip! Over went his cocoa, all over Mrs. Hall's table. "Oh no!" Nancy and I gasped and started scolding him. Mrs. Hall just said, "Hush. I'll get a rag," and fixed him another mugful.

Donald apologized and said, "If I drink a lot of this, will I turn brown like you?"

Mrs. Hall's laugh rang out like a melody. "No, baby, it don't work that way. See, God fashions folks in different colors. You'll always be a pinkish boy with cornsilk hair and sapphire eyes, and I'll always be Ol' Cocoa Skin."

After our snack, Mrs. Hall wrapped up some cookies and said, "Here's a plate for after supper. Your mama might be needin' something scrumptious, 'specially now with tryin' to keep up her energy and her milk for that littlest angel-baby." She was talking about our one-week-old brother, Christopher. Then Nancy and I practiced spelling with Mrs. Hall while Donald arranged his dinosaurs and watched cartoons.

Daddy finally called us home for the meatloaf supper he had made, and Aunt Carol was there, folding wash and dusting furniture. Momma and the baby were just waking up when we walked in, so Nancy and I didn't dare tattle on Donald. As a matter of fact, I forgot all about it till Aunt Carol set out the cookies and Donald said, "Is Mrs. Hall a nigger? Robert in my class says so."

Momma passed Christopher to Aunt Carol in one easy motion. She grabbed Donald by the arm, pulled him to the sink, and gave him a few drops of dish soap on his tongue. Donald spluttered, cried, and spat out bubbles. Aunt Carol handed Christopher to Daddy and snatched a towel from the counter. "For heaven's sake, he's only in kindergarten," she scolded Momma.

Momma held her ground. "That's why he's getting soap now, to wash that filthy word out of his mouth before he gets one day older. That way, he won't forget."

Christopher started crying, too, so Daddy got up to walk him, and I couldn't tell if Daddy agreed with Momma or with Aunt Carol. Aunt Carol helped Donald rinse his mouth, then he ran to his room. Nancy and I nibbled at the cookies, Christopher stopped crying, and Momma went to have a talk with Donald, and there was peace again.

Aunt Carol helped us set out tomorrow's clothes and we brushed our teeth. As she was getting her coat on to leave, the phone rang. Momma whispered. She listened for a moment and then went pale. She looked at Daddy. "It's Jerry," I heard her say.

Daddy took the receiver and listened, too. He shook his head, and I saw his jaw tighten. He whispered, "I'll be right there." He turned to Momma and said, "Quick, call Al Lembke and Jess Wilson. Then call the police."

Babs and Annie's fathers, I realized. But who was Jerry? Not Jerry Sullivan from my religion class. Jerry Kausner, the paperboy? Daddy took a deep breath and opened the door. Momma gave the phone to Aunt Carol and ran to the hall. "Here. Take this. Just in case." She handed Daddy a baseball bat.

Suddenly I figured it out. Geri, not Jerry. Mrs. Hall's first name was Geraldine, and Momma and Daddy called her Geri.

Aunt Carol gathered us up with her arms like a wide-winged hen protecting her chicks. She closed the drapes. Momma yanked them back open. "No, I have to see." She turned out the lights, then she opened the window.

We could hear yelling, swearing. Lots of anger. Name-calling. Over and over, the word that Momma had washed out of Donald's mouth. I felt sick to my stomach. A bitter taste rose up in my mouth. I was sure it tasted much worse than soap.

I squinted and saw my best friends' fathers running over. They had baseball bats, too. Nancy was clinging to my nightgown, and Momma had Donald in a firm grip.

We could see six younger men shaking their fists at Daddy, Mr. Lembke, and Mr. Wilson. One of them grabbed Daddy by the collar with one hand, and his other hand was balled into a hard fist. I didn't think I would ever breathe again.

Daddy surprised him with a sudden movement that pinned his arm up against his back. He raised the baseball bat. "Don't make me use this," he said in a voice I'd never heard before.

Mr. Wilson wrestled another young man to the ground, and three others sped away in an old blue Dodge as Mr. Lembke caught and cornered the remaining one against Mrs. Hall's garage. That's when two police cars screeched up, red lights flashing.

When Daddy came back into the house, he was panting, but at least he sounded like Daddy again.

"She'll be okay now. They broke some windows, but we'll board them up overnight."

I gasped. Broken windows? Chico? I thought. As if Daddy was reading my mind, he said, "Good thing the little bird was in his cage."

"Whew," Nancy and I said together.

Daddy continued, "And they spray-painted her car with hate words. Al and I will take it to the shop tomorrow."

Donald's eyes grew wide as full moons.

Mrs. Hall wouldn't come to spend the night. She said, "This here's my home. Ain't no one gonna drive me out of it."

Momma held onto Daddy's arm and laid her head on his shoulder. Aunt Carol shivered and pulled her coat around her like we were having a January blizzard. She looked at Daddy and said, "What're you, crazy, going out there?"

Daddy didn't answer right away.

"No," I blurted out then. "They're heroes. Maybe even martyrs."

Daddy walked over to me. He sighed as if all the energy was going out of him, like a balloon when somebody unties it. Then he touched my cheek like I was made of something fragile. No words. Just the touch.

Up in our beds, Nancy asked me, "Weren't you scared?"

"Terrified." I leaned against my pillow and felt really tired all of a sudden. "And something else, too," I added a moment later.

Nancy must have been asleep because she never asked about the something else. And it's a good thing because I'm not sure I could have explained it anyway.

That night I dreamed of hate and love. I dreamed of soldiers and martyrs. And especially heroes.